Original title:

Carmine Runes Along the Faerie Shed

Author: Kaido Väinamäe

ISBN HARDBACK: 978-1-80562-933-7

ISBN PAPERBACK: 978-1-80564-454-5

The Word of the Wandering Winds

In twilight's glow where shadows dance,
The winds do whisper tales of chance.
They weave through trees, in solemn flight,
Carving echoes into the night.

With laughter light and secrets spun,
They carry dreams of old and young.
Each note a fragment, soft and sweet,
Guiding lost souls with gentle beat.

Beneath the stars, the currents sigh,
A symphony beneath the sky.
They speak of places yet unseen,
Of realms where magic reigns as queen.

Through valleys low and mountains high,
They paint the world, both bold and shy.
A tapestry of hopes and fears,
That dances through the passing years.

So heed the whispers of the breeze,
And let your heart find how to seize.
For in those words of air and light,
Lies the truth of wrong and right.

The Cursed Inscriptions of Eldara

In shadows deep where secrets lie,
Ancient runes beckon, whispering why.
Their words, like thorns, pierce the night,
Cursed inscriptions, hide from the light.

A tale of woe, in parchment confined,
A lost enchantress, her heart, maligned.
With ink of sorrow, she penned her fate,
Her voice now echoes through time's cruel gate.

Beware the call of Eldara's song,
For harmony fades where curses throng.
Once you decipher, you cannot flee,
Bound to the magic of dark prophecy.

The Lore of the Gilded Glade

In the Gilded Glade where the sunlight plays,
Nature's stories weave through golden rays.
Each leaf tells tales of joy and plight,
Whispered in shadows, stitched by the light.

Beneath the boughs, the legends rest,
Of whispered dreams and hearts' behest.
A tapestry rich, imbued with time,
Where every echo resonates in rhyme.

Fairies dance in the evening's hush,
While flowers sway in a twilight rush.
Listen closely, and you may find,
The secrets of life, intertwined.

Vibrant Tales of the Cultivated Grove

In cultivated groves, where wonders grow,
Vibrant tales in the wind do flow.
With blossoms bright, they sing of grace,
In sunlit arcs, the spirits embrace.

Each sapling whispers of ancient lore,
Roots entwined, they long to explore.
Echoes of laughter and wisdom profound,
In the heart of the grove, their magic is found.

As twilight descends with a Gentle sigh,
The stars above wink, as dreams flutter by.
In every rustle, a story spins,
Of joy and sorrow, where life begins.

The Fable of Magenta Dreams

In the realm of dreams, so magenta and bright,
Where fantasies bloom in the velvet night.
Each vision a canvas, painted with care,
A fable unfolds in the perfumed air.

Waves of twilight wrap around the soul,
In this vivid land, we find our whole.
With stardust whispers that twirl and glide,
Where hopes ignite and wishes abide.

Let your heart wander in colors untamed,
In the magic of night where all is unframed.
For in every dream, we dwell and soar,
In the fable of magenta, forever we explore.

The Allure of Maple Insignia

In whispers of the autumn's glow,
The maple leaves begin to show.
Their crimson dance, a fleeting song,
In twilight hours, where dreams belong.

Beneath their boughs, the secrets twine,
Of whispered words and hopes divine.
A tapestry of fire and gold,
The stories of the brave unfold.

With every rustle, echoes call,
From ages past, through woods so tall.
Each leaf a token, softly pressed,
A magic charm in nature dressed.

The scent of earth, the kiss of air,
Awakes the soul to wonder's stare.
As twilight deepens, shadows blend,
In maple hues, the heart shall mend.

So tread with care on this soft ground,
Where every breath is magic found.
The allure draws you, cannot resist,
A spell of autumn, a lover's tryst.

Tokens of the Enchanted Artist

In hidden glades where dreams unfold,
The artist's heart, a tale retold.
With brush in hand and spirit bright,
Each stroke ignites the starry night.

A canvas waits, both blank and vast,
In colors bold, the shadows cast.
From whispers deep, the muses glean,
The magic spun, like threads of green.

With every hue, a story sings,
Of playful worlds and wondrous things.
A gentle breeze, it carries forth,
The essence of enchanted worth.

The artist's gaze, a window wide,
To realms where fanciful dreams abide.
In every stroke, a heartbeat glows,
As mystery in colors flows.

So wander close and linger here,
Among the echoes, pure and clear.
For tokens left by hands so dear,
Embrace the magic, draw it near.

Secrets Enlaced in Autumnal Lace

The crisping air, a silent sigh,
As leaves like lace in breezes fly.
With amber threads and sunlit seams,
Autumn weaves its whispering dreams.

In twilight glow, the shadows play,
Each secret kept, like night and day.
With whispered tales in every breeze,
The stories drift through rustling trees.

A tapestry of twilight hues,
In every pattern, life imbues.
The lace of autumn, soft and bright,
Embroiders warmth in fading light.

Each fallen leaf, a mem'ry spun,
Of laughter shared, of days long run.
As dusk ascends, the magic speaks,
In gentle tones, the heart it seeks.

So linger here, where tales entwine,
In nature's art, forever shine.
For secrets found in autumnal lace,
Invite the soul to find its place.

The Melody Beneath the Blossom

In gardens rich with fragrant blooms,
A melody within them looms.
The petals whisper, soft and low,
A tune of life, a gentle flow.

With every step, the notes arise,
In harmony beneath the skies.
The fragrance dances, sweet and light,
In every heart, a spark ignites.

Among the boughs, the breezes weave,
A symphony, the earth's reprieve.
Each blossom graced with nature's song,
A chorus bright, where dreams belong.

The rhythm thrums in softest hues,
Inviting joy, dispelling blues.
For in this place, the spirits soar,
The melody ignites once more.

So bask in blooms, let worries cease,
Embrace the harmony, find peace.
For in each blossom, deep and true,
The world's sweet song awaits for you.

Whispers of Petal Prose

In garden's hush, the petals sigh,
Soft secrets twirl, as breezes fly.
With ink of dew, they dance and spin,
An ancient tale where dreams begin.

Upon the breeze, a shadow drifts,
Each whisper carries nature's gifts.
The moonlight glows on leaves so fine,
While starlit paths through night entwine.

Beneath the stars, the flowers muse,
With every hue, a tale infused.
In twilight's grip, their voices blend,
As broken hearts find hope to mend.

In silence thick, the truths are laid,
In honeyed words, the stories played.
Each petal holds a memory deep,
In tranquil hours, when all is sleep.

A tapestry of scent and sight,
In blooming colors, pure delight.
As poets dream and lovers sigh,
The whispers bloom, then softly die.

The Faerie's Crimson Diary

In twilight's glow, her heart was bold,
A crimson book in hand, untold.
Each page adorned with starlit grace,
A faerie's world, a hidden place.

With ink of twilight, secrets spill,
Of moonlit dances and wishes still.
In forest's depths, where shadows play,
The echoes weave, then drift away.

A whispered charm, a silken rhyme,
Each fleeting moment, frozen time.
Her laughter twinkled with soft delight,
A lullaby to soothe the night.

Through petals pressed, emotions flow,
With every tear, a tale to sow.
In dreams she weaves her magic thread,
A tapestry of lives long fled.

The stars bear witness to her plight,
As velvet shadows cloak the night.
Amidst the wild, her heart shall soar,
The faerie's dreams forevermore.

Becoming the Nature's Narrator

Beneath the boughs, a heart does bloom,
Whispers linger in the room.
With every rustle, stories rise,
In nature's lap, the truth belies.

The brook sings songs of ages past,
While time, like shadows, swiftly casts.
In every leaf, a tale takes flight,
The narrator born of day and night.

Among the colors, deep and bright,
Each petal tells of joy and fright.
Through roots of wisdom, wisdom grows,
A silent dance, the forest knows.

With every breeze, a voice unfurls,
As nature spins her magic pearls.
In porous soil, the tales entwine,
The soul of earth, forever shine.

To listen close, the heart must glean,
For nature's voice stays ever keen.
As seasons change, new scripts are penned,
In harmony where all things blend.

From womb of earth to skies above,
In nature's chorus, we find love.
Narrators rise and tales are spun,
The story of the earth, begun.

Tales Traced in Flora's Memory

Upon the hill, where flowers sway,
The whispers of the past will play.
Each blossom holds a history rare,
In nature's book, with utmost care.

Through winding paths, the scents reek,
Where sunlight dances, so unique.
In vibrant hues, emotions sway,
As flora weaves her soft ballet.

From fields of gold to forests grand,
Each petal tells of long-lost land.
In softest lilt, the stories stir,
In rustling leaves, a gentle purr.

A tapestry of golden dreams,
In every bud, a truth redeems.
Through history's breath, the flowers sigh,
As moments fade, like clouds on high.

In tranquil glades, where soul finds peace,
The heart's longing shall never cease.
For in each bloom, a love is found,
A fragrant treasure, unbound.

The tales once told in whispered breath,
Now etched in petals, life from death.
As seasons shift and time moves on,
In flora's memory, we are reborn.

The Script of the Starry Verge

In twilight's glow, the stars align,
A script unraveled, so divine.
Whispers dart on the cool night air,
Dreams take flight, as wishes dare.

Beneath the veil of endless skies,
Ancient tales softly arise.
Each twinkle weaves a mystic thread,
To places where the brave have tread.

Celestial paths twine in delight,
Voices echo through the night.
Every glance a story spun,
Under the gaze of moon and sun.

Galaxies pulse in rhythmic beat,
Guiding souls on cosmic fleet.
The universe sings its lore,
Unfolding magic evermore.

For in this vast, enchanted frame,
We etch our hearts, ignite our flame.
With ink of stars and dreams we scribe,
On this verge, we come alive.

Inscriptions of Echoing Whimsy

In shadows cast by lantern's glow,
Echoes dance, both soft and low.
Whimsy weaves in playful strands,
Adventures bloom in enchanted lands.

Penning tales on uneven ground,
Inscriptions bright, in laughter found.
Where goblins dance and fairies play,
Lost in wonder, hearts sway.

The flutter of wings, a mystery,
In every corner, laughter free.
Each footstep stirs forgotten rhymes,
Composing joy amidst the times.

With every ink drop, whispers rise,
In fanciful voices beneath the skies.
Through twisted paths, our spirits soar,
In whimsy's arms, forevermore.

So gather 'round, let stories twine,
In echoes sweet, we shall dine.
With jubilant hearts and spirits light,
We scribe our fables into the night.

Enigma Beyond the Treeline

Within the wood, where secrets bloom,
Enigmas lurk within the gloom.
Every rustle, a tale begins,
A whispered hush where the wild kin wins.

Beneath the leaves, an ancient song,
The forest hums, both soft and strong.
Mystic shadows play their game,
In stillness, echoes call your name.

Paths untrodden beckon with grace,
Hidden wonders in every space.
With eager hearts, we search and seek,
For magic thrives where spirits speak.

The innate charm of twilight's sway,
Guiding us gently on our way.
With spark and shimmer, the night unfolds,
Revealing treasures, dreams untold.

So linger here, where mysteries call,
Beyond the treeline, heed the thrall.
In every twist and turn we find,
The enigma embraces heart and mind.

The Silhouette of Written Wishes

In the quiet dusk, wishes cling,
Silhouettes dance on delicate wing.
A tapestry woven with hopeful threads,
Each penned desire, where longing spreads.

With quill in hand, we chart our dreams,
In twilight's glow, the future gleams.
For every wish, a story untold,
A journey begins, brave and bold.

Ink flows freely, from heart to page,
Creating magic, breaking the cage.
With whispered hopes, we paint the night,
Our silhouettes bathed in silver light.

The shadows gather, secrets unfold,
Warmth in each letter, like marigold.
In every stroke, we carve our fate,
Embrace the silence, anticipate.

So send your wishes, let them fly,
In the silhouette of the moonlit sky.
For written dreams, like stars, will blaze,
Guiding our hearts through life's maze.

Glimmers of Dawn in Sylvan Silence

In quiet woods where shadows play,
The dawn awakes, a soft ballet.
With whispers low, the leaves converse,
As light spills gold, the universe.

A gentle hush, the dew drops gleam,
Each beam of light, a waking dream.
The brook sings sweet, a lilting tune,
While flowers bow beneath the moon.

The air is laced with floral breath,
Awakening life from subtle death.
In every nook, a secret stirs,
Enchanting us with all that blurred.

Beneath the boughs, sweet silence reigns,
Each moment softens, soothes our pains.
The sylvan world, a whispered charm,
Embraces all with tender balm.

As shadows dance and daylight breaks,
The forest hums, the spirit wakes.
In glimmers bright, the dawn's embrace,
We find our hearts in nature's grace.

Fables of the Charmed Glimmering Glade

In glades where secrets softly dwell,
The whispering winds weave tales to tell.
Of fae and sprites, of moonlit dreams,
In shadows deep, nothing's as it seems.

Beneath the boughs, the stories rise,
Of lovelorn hearts and wistful sighs.
Each leaf a page, each breeze a verse,
Enchanting souls, for better or worse.

The brook flows clear, a crystal song,
With notes that fashion fables long.
A tapestry of myths unspun,
In every dusk, a tale begun.

With vibrant hues, the flowers gleam,
As if awakened from a dream.
Their colors bold, their scents so sweet,
Invite the weary with gentle greet.

In light and shadow, magic braids,
The heart finds peace in nature's glades.
Where fables come alive at dusk,
And love blooms wild, a fragrant musk.

The Painted Word of Wildwood Spirits

In wildwood realms where spirits tread,
The painted word, the stories fed.
On canvas green and skies of blue,
They craft their tales, both old and new.

With brushes made of ivy's sway,
They etch the night and color the day.
Each stroke a note, each pause a sigh,
As dreams take flight, and shadows fly.

The winds carry tales of yore,
Of battles fought and lovers' lore.
In every rustle, echoes sing,
Of timeless bonds and forgotten spring.

The spirits dance 'neath ancient trees,
With laughter light as summer's breeze.
In whispers soft, their magic swirls,
Spinning dreams for boys and girls.

With painted words, they share their art,
To weave a bond, to stir the heart.
In wildwood's charm, the magic stirs,
And life unfolds in whispered murmurs.

Blossom and Flame in the Enchanted Wilds

In enchanted wilds where colors blend,
The blossom breathes, the flame will bend.
With petals bold that blush and stir,
They dance in light—a vibrant blur.

The flicker bright, a fiery glow,
In twilight's arms, the shadows flow.
Each bud a promise, each spark a dream,
In nature's heart, the rhythms teem.

The evening deep, as twilight hums,
When whispered secrets softly come.
The flowers glow, the embers wink,
With every step, the magic links.

The wilds alive with song and flame,
No two the same, yet all the same.
With every breath, we feel the call,
To cherish life, to embrace it all.

In blossom's blush and flame's delight,
We find our truths in dark and light.
The enchanted wilds, forever bright,
Awake our souls, inspire our flight.

Mysteries of the Whispering Thicket

In shadows deep where whispers dwell,
The trees keep secrets none can tell.
A flicker of light, a rustle of leaves,
Awaits the heart that truly believes.

With every breeze that steals through night,
A story unfolds, a glimmering sight.
Nimble feet dance on mossy ground,
While echoing laughter sings all around.

Moonbeams descend to touch the earth,
A coming together of magic and mirth.
Through tangled roots, adventures entwine,
In the thicket's embrace, where mysteries shine.

Messages from Crimson Blossoms

Upon the bank where roses glow,
Crimson petals tell tales of woe.
They flutter softly in twilight's embrace,
Whispering secrets of a long-lost place.

Each bloom's soft sigh carries a tune,
Of lovers lost beneath the moon.
The garden sighs, a tender heart,
Yearning for those who drifted apart.

Yet in their scent, hope's promise lies,
A fragrant reminder, as time flies.
From every blossom, a message so clear,
That love, though lost, can still linger near.

Faerie Secrets in the Scarlet Shadows

Beneath the trees where shadows creep,
Faeries weave tales while the world sleeps.
In scarlet hues, they dance with glee,
Guardians of wish and mystery.

Their laughter sparkles like stars above,
A melody of enchantment and love.
Like fleeting whispers in the breeze,
They share their secrets with ancient trees.

In twilight's glow, when silence reigns,
The heart can hear their sweet refrains.
A realm unfolds, just out of sight,
In the scarlet shadows, magic takes flight.

Inked Petals in the Woodland

In the woodland bright where dreams take flight,
Inked petals unfold in the soft twilight.
They carry tales of wonders untold,
Of knights and dragons, of courage bold.

With every brush of wind that calls,
Their stories inked on forest walls.
Woven with lore of love and fate,
These petals sing of the worlds they create.

From gentle streams to mountains high,
Each petal whispers, each turn a sigh.
In the heart of the wood, where magic prevails,
Inked petals reveal the hidden trails.

Azure Shadows in a Magenta World

In a realm where colors blend,
Azure shadows softly wend.
Whispers of secrets linger near,
Caught in dreams, forgotten fear.

The magenta sky begins to sing,
Songs of hopes and tender spring.
Glimmers dance on twilight's seam,
Bathed in warmth, a waking dream.

Hearts entwined in twilight's breath,
Life and magic intertwined, no death.
Underneath the pastel glow,
Wonders bloom, and spirits flow.

With each step, the pathway glows,
Unraveling where the river flows.
In this world, no dark to find,
Just the light, forever blind.

As shadows stretch and colors fade,
Echoes of laughter softly played.
In azure realms, our hearts will twirl,
Lost within this painted world.

Beneath the Gnarled Canopy

Under branches, old and wise,
Mysteries lurk beneath the skies.
The whispering leaves, a gentle song,
Guide the traveler ever long.

Roots entwined in tales untold,
Ancient secrets, brave and bold.
Beneath the gnarled canopy's weave,
Promises made that we believe.

Mossy carpets cradle the ground,
In every nook, enchantments found.
Shadows play and dance with light,
Where day surrenders to the night.

Flickers of magic, soft and near,
In the silence, one can hear.
A heartbeat echoing the past,
Life's fleeting moments, made to last.

So venture forth with hearts so brave,
In the woods, our spirits save.
Beneath the gnarled branches' sway,
Find your truth; let dreams not stray.

Firefly Tales from the Hidden Nook

In twilight's hush, the fireflies glow,
Little lanterns in the shadows throw.
Whispers of stories take their flight,
Dancing softly in the night.

Beneath the stars, where wishes dwell,
They flicker and weave a secret spell.
Tales of wonder flit and sway,
In hidden nooks where dreams can play.

Each glow a sign, a message clear,
From distant realms, they draw us near.
In glimmering paths, the heart will find,
Imagination unconfined.

With gentle wings, they lead the way,
Guiding lost souls who've gone astray.
Through silver threads, let hope ignite,
In the embrace of soft moonlight.

So linger here, in the still of night,
Where fireflies dance, and spirits light.
In hidden nooks, let stories bloom,
For in their glow, there's always room.

Luminous Scribbles of Lost Dreams

In the attic, shadows play,
Luminous scribbles hide away.
Tattered pages, whispers loom,
Echoes of hopes lost in the gloom.

Ink-stained fingers trace the past,
Dreams once vivid, fading fast.
The flicker of a candlelight,
Shadows twirl in the soft night.

Forgotten tales on dusty shelves,
Reflections of our former selves.
Each scribble tells a different fate,
Yearning hearts that hesitate.

In the quiet, ghosts remind,
Of the wishes left behind.
Memories linger, softly gleam,
Here among the lost, they dream.

So gather near and listen well,
To the stories only dreams can tell.
In luminous scribbles, we will find,
The spark of hope that's intertwined.

The Soft Glow of Woodland Epiphanies

In twilight's hush, the woods ignite,
With whispers soft, and dreams in flight.
A gentle breeze through branches sways,
Each leaf a secret, in twilight's gaze.

The ferns like dancers, bow and sway,
In softest green, they find their play.
A glimmer here, a spark of truth,
In nature's arms, we find our youth.

The brooklet murmurs tales of old,
Of ancient realms where magic's bold.
In shadows deep, we stroll with grace,
A journey carved in nature's embrace.

Beneath the canopies, we muse,
Among the trails we've come to choose.
Each step unveiled, the heart's delight,
A soft glow guiding through the night.

In woodland's calm, our souls align,
With every sigh, we've crossed a line.
Epiphanies in twilight's hold,
In whispered winds, our truths unfold.

Pomegranates in the Thicket's Heart

In tangled roots, the thicket lies,
With pomegranates 'neath painted skies.
Each ruby fruit a treasure's claim,
In nature's hands, they play their game.

The sunlight drapes in dusky hues,
A tapestry of reds and blues.
Upon the branches, secrets cling,
A sweet embrace from autumn's wing.

Each burst of juice, a story spills,
Of ancient lands and rolling hills.
The thicket's heart, a sacred place,
Where time dissolves, and dreams embrace.

From narrow paths, we wander near,
With every step, a softened cheer.
The laughter shared, the sun's warm kiss,
In pomegranates, we find our bliss.

In twilight's glow, the echoes start,
Of harvest's joy, within the heart.
In every seed, a world anew,
The thicket's charm, forever true.

When the Wild Roses Speak

When wild roses softly sigh,
A gentle breeze will drift nearby.
Their petals whisper secrets sweet,
In fragrant blooms, where lovers meet.

Beneath the arch of verdant green,
In daylight's glow, such beauty seen.
They sway like dancers, bold and free,
A language pure, unbound, and free.

With thorns that guard their velvet grace,
They paint the path we dare to trace.
With every blush, they tell a tale,
Of tender hearts that will prevail.

In twilight's hush, they lean and sigh,
As fireflies weave a dance nearby.
Their fragrance lingers, rich and near,
A symphony that draws us near.

When wild roses call, we must attend,
To hear the truths that never end.
In petals soft, the world awakes,
In every whisper, love partakes.

A Symphony in Gilded Shadows

In gilded shadows, melodies play,
As twilight drapes the end of day.
Each note a glimmer, soft and clear,
A symphony that draws us near.

The trees sway gently, keeping time,
As nature weaves her secret rhyme.
In every rustle, every breeze,
The music hums among the leaves.

With whispered chords, the night unfolds,
A tapestry of stories told.
The stars, like lanterns, shine so bright,
Illuminating paths in night.

In dreams and shadows, hearts will blend,
To dance where night and magic mend.
A symphony, both wild and grand,
We find our place, hand in hand.

In every silence, there is song,
A rhythm deep where we belong.
In gilded shadows, let us roam,
For this is where we find our home.

Beneath the Blushing Canopy

In the wood where shadows play,
Leaves whisper secrets of the day.
Sunlight dances, filters through,
A world alive, in vibrant hue.

Mushrooms bloom with a gentle grace,
While fairies flit in their hidden space.
Every rustle, a magic tune,
Beneath the blush of the afternoon.

Old oaks stand with wise embrace,
Guardians of this enchanted place.
Roots like veins, deep and profound,
Heartbeats echo in the ground.

With each breeze comes a story spun,
Of battles fought, and loves begun.
Beneath the canopy's softly swayed
Whispers of dreams the forest made.

Here, in this realm, the wild holds tight,
A spell woven in morning light.
Under the sky, a tapestry glows,
Tales of wonder that only nature knows.

Traces of the Enchanted Scribe

In the quiet nook of a timeworn shop,
Dust motes shimmer, as memories hop.
Ink stains pool on the faded page,
Life's enduring script in a golden cage.

Quills dance lightly, trace a spell,
Stories woven like a secret well.
Underneath the moon's pale watch,
Pages flutter as dreamers scotch.

Words of wisdom, wrapped in lore,
Echo softly, forevermore.
In every letter, a heartbeat sings,
Binding fate with delicate strings.

The scribe, a shadow in candlelight,
Crafts a world that takes its flight.
With every stroke, the past reveals,
A magic grasp that softly steals.

And when the sun bids a farewell glow,
The ink surrenders to twilight's flow.
Traces linger in the still of night,
On parchment dreams, in whispered light.

Vermilion Letters in the Dawn

At dawn's first blush, a letter speaks,
In vermilion hues, the heart it seeks.
Quivering promises on wings take flight,
As hope awakens in morning's light.

Each stroke of the pen, a gentle sigh,
Carved in silence, where secrets lie.
The sun unfurls a shimmering thread,
Binding souls with the words unsaid.

A breeze carries whispers of the day,
Where dreams and memories softly sway.
With each heartbeat, the rhythm grows,
In the dance of love, the spirit flows.

Vermilion letters, kissed by the sun,
Stories of two, now forever spun.
In the history etched on this sacred sheet,
Fate's melody plays, forever sweet.

As shadows linger, the dawn unfolds,
In letters bright, the truth beholds.
A promise painted in the sky's embrace,
Two souls entwined in the sacred space.

Reflections of an Almond Tree's Heart

Beneath the boughs of an ancient tree,
Whispers of wisdom drift lazily.
Almond blossoms flutter, soft and white,
Hiding laughter from morning's light.

The bark bears witness to ages past,
Stories of lovers, spells cast.
Roots entwined deep in the earth,
Echoing tales of wonder and worth.

Every rustle tells of dreams grown shy,
Of moments fleeting as time drifts by.
The heart of the tree, golden and true,
Reflects the wonder in all it knew.

In spring's embrace, the petals unfold,
A tapestry woven with stories bold.
Sunlight dapples on tender green,
In each rustle, a life unseen.

As dusk descends with a silver hue,
The almond tree dreams of the past it knew.
In reflections soft, its heart beats slow,
Cradling secrets only the moon can know.

Harmonies of the Wildflower's Heart

In meadows bright where wildflowers sway,
The whispers of the gentle breeze play.
Colors dance in sunlight's warm embrace,
Nature's symphony fills every space.

Petals brush against a curious bee,
While tales unfold beneath the great oak tree.
Moments captured in blossoms' soft hue,
Each one a secret, known to just a few.

With every flutter of wings in flight,
The dance of the garden ignites pure delight.
Awakening dreams as dusk paints the sky,
In the heart of the wildflower, nothing can die.

Echoes linger where shadows softly fall,
Voices of nature beckon and call.
In the wildflower's heart, stories entwine,
As time weaves its magic, sublime and divine.

Writing the Forgotten Forest's Story

In the depths of the forest where silence reigns,
Ancient whispers echo like forgotten trains.
Each rustling leaf tells tales of the past,
Of heroes and dreams that forever last.

Mossy stones bear inscriptions of old,
Woven yarns of adventures waiting to be told.
With quill in hand, on parchment so bare,
The spirits of woodland rise up from their lair.

The moon spills silver on pathways unseen,
Charting the paths that linger between.
Writing the stories that cover each nook,
As shadows and stars weave the pages they took.

With every word, a life is reborn,
In the embrace of the forest, forlorn.
Together we sketch the echoes of yore,
In whispers of leaves, the past we restore.

Whispers of the Fabled Grove

Deep in the grove where the legends lie,
Ancestors' voices in the branches comply.
Their tales intertwine with the rustling leaves,
In a language that hums what the heart believes.

Soft twilight descends with its shimmering glow,
As fireflies twinkle, a beckoning show.
With each whispered secret that dances on air,
The magic of old weaves through dreams laid bare.

Beneath the old willow, shadows unite,
Fables of courage flicker with light.
The ground holds the footprints of those who dared,
To chase down the dreams that night never scared.

In the fabled grove, where time sways and bends,
All stories converge, where beginnings and ends.
With each silent tear and joyous refrain,
The whispers of wisdom echo like rain.

The Goldleaf Chronicles

In the shimmer of autumn, sweet gold leaves fall,
Chronicles written by nature's soft call.
Each leaf a tale of change and delight,
A saga of seasons, so vivid, so bright.

Carved by the winds of a world so alive,
The drama of nature helps the heart strive.
With murmurs of life in the cool, crisp air,
The goldleaf chronicles dance without care.

Beneath the vast sky where the eagles soar,
Each fluttering page opens a new door.
In whispers of rustle, futures are born,
As the tapestry weaves with each whispered dawn.

From laughter of squirrels to the hush of the night,
The goldleaf chronicles hold dreams in their flight.
In every soft landing, in every bright hue,
Each moment encaptured in a tale made true.

Secrets Written in Berry Stains

In the shadows where whispers dwell,
Berries spill secrets no tongue can tell.
With crimson juice on parchment pressed,
A tale of longing, a heart's restless quest.

The moonlight dances on leaves so green,
As ancient dreams weave through the unseen.
A rustle here, a sigh escapes,
In berry stains, the magic shapes.

Hidden paths where the wild things roam,
Marking the journey, the call of home.
With every drop, a story's spun,
In berry stains, the lost are won.

Beneath the thick canopy, shadows play,
In the heart of the forest, night consumes day.
Whispers of the past linger with grace,
In berry stains, we find our place.

Chronicles of the Glade's Emissaries

Through the glade where the wild winds sift,
Emissaries gather, nature's gift.
With threads of light in their gentle hands,
They weave the tales of enchanted lands.

Every creature knows their silent call,
From feathered friends to the grand oak tall.
In harmony, they share their lore,
Guardians of secrets, forevermore.

Moonlit nights bring them into view,
To dance with shadows, both old and new.
With whispers soft as the starlit breeze,
They pledge their vows beneath ancient trees.

Together they stitch the fabric of dreams,
In the glade where nothing is as it seems.
Every heartbeat is a promise made,
In this sanctuary, light and shade.

When morning breaks, they fade away,
Leaving only echoes of their play.
But in the hearts of those who believe,
The chronicles of hope never leave.

Glyphs of the Enshrouded Grove

In the grove where silence reigns,
Glyphs are etched in ancient veins.
Whispers of wisdom, carved in stone,
A language of nature, a truth to be known.

Through twisted branches, the sunlight weaves,
Telling stories of what the fir tree believes.
Each symbol a portal, a tale to explore,
In the dance of the leaves, secrets galore.

When shadows stretch in the fading light,
The glyphs glow softly, revealing the night.
With every flicker, a story unfolds,
Of warriors, lovers, and destinies bold.

Intra the hush, one hears the call,
Of forgotten lore hidden in the sprawl.
Every step taken, a path to divining,
In this enchanted haven, old stars aligning.

So linger a while in the grove's warm embrace,
Let the glyphs guide you to forgotten space.
In the heart of the forest, magic's alive,
By these markings of old, our spirits will thrive.

Threads of Vermilion Wishes

Woven in twilight, a tapestry gleams,
Threads of vermilion dance with dreams.
Each strand a hope, a wish to unfurl,
A universe crafted, a sparkling swirl.

The fabric of fate in gentle hands molds,
With tales of enchantment, brave and bold.
In the depths of the night, wishes take flight,
Carried like whispers on the wings of the night.

Stitched by the moon, through shadows they tread,
Embracing the light, where the heart's led.
On the loom of the stars, they twine and bend,
Creating a story where journeys ascend.

Through valleys of solace and peaks of despair,
They traverse the silence, a tender prayer.
With every thread, they weave the divine,
In vermilion hues, hearts intertwine.

So breathe in the magic, let your wishes ignite,
In the tapestry woven beneath the starlight.
With threads of vermilion, your dreams take their stand,
In the great scheme of life, a woven strand.

Coral Hues in Twilight's Embrace

As evening drapes with coral light,
The whispers dance in fading sight.
Where shadows stretch and dreams take flight,
Magic glimmers in the night.

Beneath a sky of molten gold,
The secrets of the dusk unfold.
In every breeze, a tale retold,
Of wonders waiting to be bold.

Soft waves murmur on the shore,
Calling forth the lost once more.
Each gentle ripple, ancient lore,
In twilight's arms, we yearn for more.

A canvas brushed in hues so bright,
Embraced by warmth, we lose our fright.
In this embrace, the world's delight,
Is painted in the fading light.

To wander here is to be free,
In coral hues, our spirits see.
The twilight sings of what can be,
As magic stirs like whispered tea.

Tales of the Forgotten Sylphs

In the glade where shadows play,
The sylphs of old come out to stay.
Their laughter echoes, soft and gay,
In hidden realms, they slip away.

With wings like gossamer so fine,
They weave through branches, twist and twine.
In twilight's blush, their secrets shine,
A dance of grace, a tale divine.

Once they spoke in songs of yore,
Each note a key, each verse a door.
To realms uncharted, evermore,
Where dreams and fantasies explore.

Forgotten now by time's cruel hand,
Yet echoes linger in the land.
In whispered winds, we understand,
The stories lost, we grasp, we stand.

So let us listen, hearts alight,
To tales that shimmer in the night.
For in each sylph's enchanting flight,
Lies magic waiting to ignite.

The Ruby Veil of the Sylvan Sanctuary

In woods where emerald shadows weave,
A ruby veil, a tale to cleave.
The sanctuary's heart, a reprieve,
In pulses soft, the magic grieves.

Worn by time, yet brightly glows,
Each thread of ruby gently flows.
Where whispered secrets, silence knows,
And every heartache softly shows.

A place where ancient echoes dwell,
And every leaf a story tells.
In silence rich, the spirits spell,
The dreams we cast, the fears we quell.

Within this realm of twilight's grace,
The ruby veil, a warm embrace.
In every corner, time and space,
Meld into one, a hidden place.

To wander here is pure delight,
Beneath the stars, the world feels right.
In sylvan bliss, in love's sweet sight,
We find our peace, the heart takes flight.

Secrets Woven in Moss and Moonlight

Beneath the boughs, in gentle gloom,
The moss unfolds, a soft perfume.
In moonlight's glow, old shadows loom,
And nature sings, a sweetened tune.

Secrets linger in the air,
Whispers carried without a care.
In every glance, a treasure rare,
A tapestry, textures laid bare.

The moon bestows its silver sheen,
On hidden paths where few have been.
In silence deep, the woods convene,
Where magic thrives, and hearts are keen.

Woven softly into dreams,
Are moonlit laughs and gentle beams.
In every nook, a story seems,
To surge with life, like rushing streams.

So heed the call of night's embrace,
Where secrets spark and shadows chase.
In moss and moonlight, find your place,
And let the magic softly trace.

Fluttering Threads of Magenta Mystique

In twilight's embrace, the threads do weave,
A tapestry glows, none would believe.
Soft whispers call from the distant glow,
Where dreams intertwine, and starlight flows.

Chasing the echoes of laughter near,
With colors that dance, so vivid, so clear.
The magenta hues pulse like a heart,
Binding the shadows, each twist a part.

Moonlit secrets hide in plain sight,
Fleeting moments that spark delight.
As time spins softly in twilight's loom,
The fabric breathes life, dispelling gloom.

Mysterious figures glide on the breeze,
Woven tales flutter with effortless ease.
In clouds of color, they find their way,
Guided by whispers of night into day.

So track the threads that shimmer and sway,
Unlock the magic, let your spirit play.
For in every stitch, a story's spun,
In the heart of the night, you'll find your fun.

Enigmas Shimmering in Fae Light

Beneath the moon's watch, where enchantments dwell,
The fae weave mysteries, casting their spell.
With glimmers that dance on the edge of sight,
They twirl through shadows, in fleeting flight.

In leaves of gold, their secrets unfold,
Tales of the ancients, both timeless and bold.
Each shimmer reveals a story untold,
Of realms lost to time, of treasures of old.

The laughter that echoes in crystalline streams,
Holds all the magic born from our dreams.
Glimpse the unknown, let your heart take wing,
In fae light's embrace, feel the joy it brings.

Through dappled glens where the wildflowers grow,
Whispers entice you to follow, to know.
An enigma awaits in the softest of sighs,
As the night draws near, and the day gently dies.

So step lightly forth, with reverence and grace,
Unlock the enchantments of this sacred place.
For within the fae light, secrets ignite,
And mysteries shimmer, forever in sight.

Whispers of the Celestial Garden

In the garden of stars, where dreams take flight,
Whispers woven in silken light.
Each petal a world, each leaf a tale,
Of cosmic wonders, both soft and frail.

Through cosmic blooms, where galaxies sweep,
The echoes of silence invite us to leap.
With each gentle breeze, the cosmos sighs,
As stardust collects in our wide-open eyes.

The moon's tender gaze wraps us in peace,
In this tranquil haven, all worries cease.
Soak in the magic, let your heart sing,
For the celestial whispers create endless spring.

Dance with the comets, twirl with the night,
In the glow of the heavens, our spirits take flight.
Each moment a jewel, each star a song,
In the whispers of beauty, we find we belong.

So venture within this celestial embrace,
Where wonders await in a timeless space.
For in the garden of stars, forever we'll roam,
As whispers of wonder lead us back home.

Beacons of the Berry-Laden Boughs

In boughs of berry, where sweetness resides,
The heart of the forest, where joy abides.
Amidst splashes of color, a feast for the eyes,
Beneath broad canopies, where magic lies.

The laughter of children, the rustle of leaves,
Weave tales of wonder that nature believes.
With each cherished moment, a memory grows,
In the shade of the branches, each heart freely flows.

A tapestry rich with the hues of delight,
Fills every heart with shimmering light.
From the ripest of berries to the softest of sighs,
Each beacon of beauty in silence complies.

As sunlight drips down like honeyed cheeks,
The comfort of nature softly speaks.
With hands outstretched, we gather the sweet,
In the berry-laden boughs, where life feels complete.

So wander the paths of this lush, vibrant earth,
Embrace every blessing, appreciate worth.
For in whispers of nature, we find our way,
In beacons of berries, we live, we play.

Rune Trails in a Moonlit Haven

Beneath the silver glow of night,
Shadows weave through ancient trees,
Whispers of the past take flight,
Guided by the gentle breeze.

Crimson leaves in twilight's gaze,
Mark the runes of tales untold,
Echoes of forgotten days,
Secrets that the night enfold.

Luminous paths where spirits tread,
Guide the wandering hearts anew,
With every step, a dream is fed,
In a haven where magic grew.

Stars above in silent cheer,
Bathe the world in endless light,
Calling forth the souls so dear,
To dance within the blissful night.

As dawn approaches, dreams will fade,
Yet whispers linger on the breeze,
In moonlit havens, love is made,
A tapestry of memories.

Stories of Oaken Guardians

In the heart of the enchanted wood,
Stand the guardians, strong and wise,
Ancient oaks in solemn mood,
Beneath the ever-changing skies.

Their gnarled arms embrace the night,
Cradling tales of ages past,
Of brave souls who stood for light,
And in their shadows, memories cast.

Through branches thick, the starlight beams,
Illumining the paths they guard,
Whispered hopes and woven dreams,
In each knot, a story scarred.

With rustling leaves, they softly share,
The laughter, the tears, the silent fears,
A bond of love beyond compare,
Enduring through the passing years.

In twilight's glow, their strength prevails,
Oaken giants, steadfast, true,
Guardians of both heart and tales,
In their embrace, the world renews.

Scarlet Threads of Celestial Loom

In the quiet of the twilight hour,
Threads of crimson weave the sky,
Fingers of fate in each flower,
Beneath the stars, where dreams can fly.

With every pulse, the cosmos hums,
A melody of night and day,
Spinning tales as the stillness comes,
In a softly, flowing ballet.

Woven deep within the night,
The scarlet threads of stories blend,
Each twinkle holds a spark of light,
A promise where the shadows end.

The tapestry of hopes and fears,
Drapes around the moon's bright gleam,
Harvesting laughter, love, and tears,
In the fabric of a dream.

When dawn breaks forth, the colors fade,
But echoes of the magic stay,
In every heart, a song is made,
Of scarlet threads that guide the way.

The Dance of the Dew-Kissed Petals

At dawn's first light, the petals sway,
In a gentle waltz with the breeze,
Dew-kissed dreams greet the new day,
Whispering secrets to the trees.

Each bloom a tale of vibrant hue,
Dancing in the early sun's glow,
Embracing life in every dew,
In a world where magic flows.

Fluttering wings of the morning lark,
Join the dance in joyous flight,
As petals shimmer, pure and stark,
In the orchestra of daylight.

Nature's song, in harmony,
Sings of love and gentle grace,
A woven spell of unity,
In this enchanted, sacred space.

As the sun swiftly climbs the sky,
The dance transforms, a new refrain,
Yet in each heart, the echoes lie,
Of dew-kissed petals, joy, and pain.

The Harmony of Gossamer Traces

In twilight's glow, the dreams unspool,
Whispers of fate in each shimmering drool.
Threads of silver, spun with grace,
Dancing lightly in a hidden place.

Stars awake, in silence they weave,
Stories of old, their secrets they leave.
Breezes carry the tales untold,
In unity formed, with hearts bold.

Moon's soft light, a guiding hand,
Leads us gently, through shadowed land.
In fragile webs of thought and time,
We find our rhythm, our secret rhyme.

Nature's canvas, painted light,
With colors bright, banishing night.
Harmony sings in every breath,
A melody of life, beyond death.

Together we weave, with threads so fine,
A tapestry where our spirits intertwine.
In gossamer traces, we discover our song,
In the heart of magic, we all belong.

Blessings Inscribed in Fern Fronds

In emerald whispers, soft and low,
Fern fronds dance in a gentle flow.
Each curve and twist, a story to tell,
Of ancient forests where secrets dwell.

Beneath the canopy, shadows play,
A world alive in a fresh bouquet.
Sunlight trickles through each green lace,
Lighting the paths in nature's embrace.

With every heartbeat, the earth aligns,
In sacred scripts, the essence shines.
Moments framed in delicate leaves,
In blessings inscribed, the heart believes.

Raindrops shimmer, jewels on the floor,
The rhythm of life calls us to explore.
In every fern, a promise, a sign,
A fleeting glimpse of the divine.

Embrace the ferns, their spirit so pure,
In wisdom wrapped, they quietly endure.
Nature's blessings in each gentle frond,
In every whisper, we grow strong.

The Elegy of Silken Patterns

In twilight's hush, the silence sighs,
A tapestry weaves as daylight dies.
Silken patterns, woven with care,
Echo the stories lost in the air.

Fragile beauties, soft and rare,
Countless moments, spun with despair.
Each thread a memory, woven tight,
Colors of joy fade into night.

Nature's loom, it bends and sways,
Crafting the dawn of forgotten days.
Patterns of life, both lost and found,
In every fold, our hearts resound.

An elegy sung to the fading light,
Of dreams and whispers taking flight.
With every stitch, the past entwined,
In silken patterns, our fates aligned.

As shadows gather, the tales repeat,
In woven fabric, we find our beat.
Embrace the echoes, the stories shared,
In every thread, our souls laid bare.

Messages Beneath the Canopy's Embrace

Beneath the canopy, where shadows creep,
Messages rustle, secrets they keep.
The leaves are scribes of nature's song,
In each gentle flutter, we all belong.

In whispers carried by the soft, sweet breeze,
The world is cradled in ancient trees.
Every rustling leaf, a note in flight,
A symphony born in the deepening night.

Through branches twining, a dance of fate,
The cosmos smiles on dreams that wait.
Underneath the weight of sky's embrace,
Together we wander, in this sacred space.

The heart of the forest, pulsing with life,
Breathes in rhythms of joy and strife.
In every shadow, the light takes form,
A tender message, a brewing storm.

In unity, souls gather as one,
Sending their dreams to the setting sun.
Messages spoken in nature's soft grace,
In every step, a journey we trace.

Inscriptions Among the Mossy Stones

Beneath the canopy, shadows dance,
Whispers of ages, caught in a trance.
Ancient runes nestle on earth's breast,
Guardians of secrets, in silence, they rest.

A brook sings softly, its lyrics unclear,
Carving the silence, beckoning near.
Every stone tells tales of the past,
Roots intertwine them, a bond that will last.

Moss wraps the edges, lush and alive,
In the green shadows, the spirits thrive.
Each gust of the breeze, a gentle embrace,
The stones gleam like jewels, time's tender grace.

Legends are breathing, within nature's clay,
Inscriptions of moments that fade not away.
With each footfall, the echoes revive,
Whispers of long-lost tales still survive.

In the heart of the forest, where dreams intertwine,
The mossy stones wait, old wonders align.
Seek out their magic, let your heart roam,
For among ancient markers, you'll find a home.

The Secret Melody of Sapphire Leaves

In the stillness of twilight, a song runs deep,
Sapphire leaves shimmer, as daylight sleeps.
Rustling softly, in hushed reverie,
Melodies weave through the branches, carefree.

Each leaf a note, in a symphonic breeze,
Dancing with whispers, in rhythmic ease.
Harmonies twinkle in the silvered air,
Secrets of nature, enchantingly rare.

The twilight grows richer, shadows entwined,
In the heart of the forest, what wonders you'll find.
Listen closely, hear the foliage sigh,
The song of the leaves, under starlit sky.

Moonlight cascades like a waterfall bright,
Turning the sapphire into silken light.
Each flutter and rustle, a tale to unfold,
Of ancients and magic, in whispers retold.

In this serene haven, where dreams are spun,
The secret melody plays on, never done.
Let the sapphire leaves guide your heart true,
In harmony's cradle, all skies are blue.

Legends of the Scarlet Spires

Up in the mountains, bold and proud,
Scarlet spires pierce the skies, enshrouded.
Legends linger in the crisp mountain air,
Whispers of adventurers, daring and rare.

They speak of a treasure, buried in time,
Hidden in shadows, a climber's steep climb.
Echoes of bravery flare in the night,
Under the glow of the hearth's flickering light.

Seasons will change, yet the stories remain,
Of hearts dared to wander, through joy and pain.
The crimson towers stand, steadfast and tall,
Witnesses to triumphs, fate's wondrous call.

Mists wrap the spires, a mystical veil,
Concealing the secrets of each storied trail.
Through valleys and thickets, the daring will roam,
For the legends of scarlet will lead them back home.

So gather your courage, let hope be your guide,
Tread on the pathways where dreams coincide.
The scarlet spires beckon, adventure awaits,
In the heart of the mountains, destiny waits.

The Echoes of Earthy Whispers

In the realm of shadows, the earth does murmur,
Echoes of whispers, in the glow of the firmer.
Beneath the surface, stories reside,
Of epochs and beings, who once walked beside.

The wind carries tales of the ancient and wise,
Through the rustling grass, where the innocence lies.
Nature pens verses, each twirl and each bend,
Scripting the saga of life without end.

Every stone and twig holds a voice of its own,
A symphony of memories, deeply sown.
With gentle persistence, the earth will unfold,
The echoes of whispers, in layers of gold.

Listen intently, for the forest knows all,
Of the quiet moments, both mighty and small.
The dance of the leaves, the song of the brook,
Are chapters of wisdom, just waiting, like books.

In the hush of the twilight, the echoes will soar,
Calling to those who yearn to explore.
For in every whisper, there's magic to trace,
And the earthy reflections will lead to solace.

The Archivo of Nature's Reverie

In twilight's grasp, the whispers soar,
Through leafy paths, they gently pour.
A tapestry of secrets spun,
Beneath the watchful, waking sun.

With each soft breeze, a tale is told,
Of ancient trees and hearts of gold.
Their shadows dance on mossy ground,
In every nook, enchantments found.

The brook sings clear, a crystal verse,
Reflecting dreams both blessed and cursed.
Its murmurs weave through roots and stone,
A symphony of the unknown.

As petals blush in morning light,
They cradle dreams of day and night.
A silent pact in nature's lore,
Where every sigh unlocks the door.

In every leaf, a story glows,
Of sunlight's warmth and midnight's throes.
The archive waits, both proud and free,
For curious souls who yearn to see.

Dreams Laid Bare Under Canopy

Beneath the arch of emerald leaves,
Where shadows play and daylight weaves,
A world awakes to whispered dreams,
In golden light, the fabric gleams.

With each soft rustle of the bough,
A promise held, a solemn vow.
To cradle secrets, lost yet found,
In nature's arms, both safe and sound.

The painted skies of dusk and dawn,
Bring forth the magic that goes on.
In the stillness, hearts align,
As moonlight spills, a silver line.

Dreams flutter like the butterflies,
In colors bright, they mesmerize.
Each flit and flutter, a story spun,
A dance of life, forever run.

So linger here, beneath the shade,
Where dreams are real and fears do fade.
In the canopy's embrace, we find,
The echoes of a timeless grind.

The Flora's Inked Secrets

In pages bound by nature's hand,
The flora writes where few can stand.
Each petal holds a verse profound,
Of life and loss, in silence drowned.

With roots like whispers in the earth,
They share the tales of love and birth.
In shadows cast by ancient trees,
Their secrets drift upon the breeze.

The ink of dusk paints every leaf,
In hues of joy, in strokes of grief.
A biography of breath and time,
In every bloom, a hidden rhyme.

Amidst the thorns and velvet blooms,
An elegance that sweetly looms.
The whispers of the wild unfurl,
In nature's arms, a mystic whirl.

So wander soft through tangled trails,
Where every scent and color hails,
The flora's ink, a legacy,
For those who seek what's yet to see.

Radiant Chronicles in the Night

As twilight falls, the stars awake,
With stories bright, they gently break.
In silver beams, their whispers gleam,
A radiant chorus, a shared dream.

The moon, a guardian up high,
Watches o'er the world, the sigh.
Each shadow casts a tale anew,
Of wanderers and paths they drew.

The nightingale begins to sing,
Of dreams that flutter, hearts take wing.
In velvet dark, the magic stirs,
In every note, the universe purrs.

With glances exchanged in silent grace,
The world transforms, a tender place.
In secret glades, by flickering light,
The radiant chronicles ignite.

So gather 'neath the starry dome,
Where every heart can find a home.
In every glow, in every spark,
The stories bloom within the dark.

Crimson Whispers in Enchanted Grove

In the heart of the twilight, shadows creep,
Whispers of magic, where secrets seep.
Crimson leaves flutter with whispers so light,
Dancing like fireflies, embracing the night.

Moss carpets the ground, soft as a sigh,
Beneath the old trees, where memories lie.
Chronicles woven in silken thread,
Each pulse of the forest, where dreams are fed.

Flickers of starlight weave through the air,
Illuminating paths that lead to somewhere rare.
Crimson reflections in pools of deep thought,
In this enchanted grove, our souls are sought.

Voices of ancients, a melodic refrain,
Calling us gently, through joy and through pain.
With moments suspended, like jewels on a string,
In each whispered echo, the forest will sing.

So linger a while, in the depths of this place,
Find solace within, wrapped in nature's grace.
Where crimson whispers and dreams intertwine,
In the warmth of the grove, let your spirit shine.

Secrets of the Verdant Glade

Glistening dew on leaves at dawn,
Secrets of nature softly drawn.
In the verdant glade, where shadows caress,
Each hidden wonder, a timeless bless.

Beneath the boughs, where silence thrives,
A tapestry woven, the magic survives.
Caterpillars transform, their stories untold,
In every hushed moment, new journeys unfold.

Rippling brook sings a gentle tune,
Carrying tales beneath the moon.
Sunbeams dance lightly on emerald seas,
Whispers of promises carried by breeze.

Secrets concealed in petals of green,
In the heartbeat of nature, they're silently seen.
With each rustling leaf, a soft-hearted plea,
A call to the wanderer, wild and free.

In the lush verdant, where shadows play,
Ancient spirits and dreams might sway.
Let the secrets untangle, take root in your soul,
In the heart of the glade, you'll find yourself whole.

Echoes of the Scarlet Light

When the dusk awakens, shadows grow long,
Echoes of scarlet weave through the song.
The horizon blushes, in hues of desire,
Igniting the sky with a shimmering fire.

Every fluttering wing, a whisper so sweet,
Lacing the twilight with soft, gentle beat.
In the dance of the day, as it softly departs,
Scarlet flames flicker, igniting our hearts.

Wisps of the past in the cool evening air,
Unraveling stories, both vivid and rare.
With each fading sunbeam, a tale unveiled,
In echoes of light, where hope has prevailed.

The horizon embraces the night's soft refrain,
Wrapping the world in a luminous chain.
Boundless and fleeting, the moments take flight,
In the echoes of scarlet, pure magic ignites.

So linger a moment and breathe in the glow,
The whispers of twilight that ebb and flow.
In the embrace of the dusk, find solace and right,
For life's sweetest secrets are present in light.

The Glistening Path of Ember Leaves

Autumn's bright ember, a tapestry spun,
Leaves dressed in gold 'til the day is done.
Each crackle beneath, a sonorous delight,
On paths that are painted with fiery light.

Whispers of wind in the branches above,
Carry the tales of the seasons we love.
With every step taken, a story unfolds,
Ember leaves shimmer with secrets untold.

The golden sunlight breaks through the trees,
Glistening pathways that beckon with ease.
Each twist and each turn leads to adventure,
In the heart of the woods lies a treasure to venture.

As shadows grow long and the day fades away,
The path glows in crimson, leading astray.
With courage ignited, embrace the unknown,
On this glistening path, you are never alone.

So wander through whispers, let wonders arrive,
In the heart of the forest, where dreams come alive.
For every ember leaves a trace of its heart,
In the magic of nature, the beauty will start.

The Kiss of Reddish Twilight

In the hush of the fading light,
Crimson whispers dance in flight,
Beneath the boughs, where secrets weave,
A kiss bestowed, we dare to believe.

The sky ignites with shades of fire,
Promises tethered, hearts aspire,
Twilight wraps the world so tight,
Holding dreams 'til day meets night.

Every shadow flutters free,
In the realm of fantasy,
We chase the remnants of the past,
In twilight's grip, the spell is cast.

Through silken strands of dusk's caress,
Magic lingers, hearts confess,
As stars emerge, the night unfolds,
In whispers soft, our truth beholds.

So linger long in twilight's glow,
Where dreams and twilight's kisses flow,
For in this moment, time stands still,
A sacred bond, a whispered thrill.

Shadows of the Scribed Sylvan

In the woods where letters breathe,
Ancient tales their magic wreathe,
Shadows dance on every tree,
Whispers echo, wild and free.

Pages flutter in the breeze,
Chasing secrets, coaxing keys,
With ink of starlight, spirits call,
Tales of wonder, binding all.

Beneath the moon's soft, watchful eye,
The stories rise and never die,
In every shadow, legends grow,
Subtle truths that ebb and flow.

Roots tell tales of days gone by,
Of loss and joy, a timeless sigh,
Through sylvan whispers, wisdom flows,
A tapestry of life that knows.

So linger here, in twilight's realm,
Where dreams and nature's hands do helm,
The scribed sylvan's heartbeat sings,
In every rustling branch, it clings.

Hues of Enchantment Unfurled

Brushstrokes bright, the world awakes,
In vibrant shades, the heart remakes,
Every hue, a story spun,
In twilight's canvas, magic's begun.

Petals stretch on winding vines,
Colors mingle, destiny aligns,
With gentle whispers, soft and warm,
Each bloom a token, a charming charm.

Through forests deep, and rivers wide,
In every color, dreams abide,
Hues of magic, dancing light,
In this enchanted, tender night.

The sky becomes a painter's dream,
With swirls of gold and silver gleam,
Each stroke a wish upon the air,
Landscapes rich, beyond compare.

As day takes flight on twilight's wing,
The colors hum, the spirits sing,
In every shade, a promise sworn,
In hues of hope, the dawn is born.

The Language of Wild Blossoms

In the whispering breeze they sway,
Wild blossoms speak in hues of gray,
Their language soft, a gentle breeze,
A tale of love among the trees.

Petals flutter, secrets shared,
In sunlight's warmth, their hearts laid bare,
Each color sings, a fragrant song,
In nature's choir, we all belong.

The wildflowers weave a fragrant lore,
Of laughter, longing, and so much more,
Each bloom a story, fierce and bright,
In wild tongues, they claim the night.

Amongst the thorns, their beauty glows,
In valleys deep, where no one goes,
They whisper wisdom, pure and true,
In every blossom, life anew.

So wander slow where wild blooms grow,
Let their soft language gently flow,
For in their dance, the earth reveals,
The timeless truth that nature heals.

Whispers of Crimson Ink

In shadows deep, the secrets flow,
Like whispers soft, where few dare go.
A quill in hand, the stories weave,
Of magic lost, and hearts that grieve.

The parchment waits, so white and pure,
To capture dreams that long endure.
With every stroke, a tale unfolds,
Of daring hearts and treasures bold.

Beneath the stars, a world awakes,
Where nothing's sure, and fate it takes.
A flicker here, a shadow there,
The ink it darkens, pulls the air.

In every line, a spark of flame,
A name long lost, a whispered claim.
With crimson's touch, the past revived,
And in those words, the heart's contrived.

So pen your thoughts, let silence break,
For every word is a choice to make.
The stories call, so heed their link,
And find your place in crimson ink.

Enchanted Marks Beneath Moonlit Boughs

In the glade where shadows dance,
The moonbeams cast a silver trance.
Beneath the boughs, the whispers sigh,
As secrets of the night drift by.

Ancient runes in mossy seams,
Awake the thoughts of long-lost dreams.
With every heartbeat, magic swells,
In tales that trees and silence tell.

The gentle breeze begins to play,
Enticing stars to come and stay.
While faerie lights in circles twine,
Their laughter weaves a sacred line.

As fingers trace the paths of fate,
The forest stirs, no longer late.
In quietude, the world reveals,
The depth of dreams that night conceals.

So linger here and feel the glow,
Of endless nights where magic flows.
With every breath, let wonder swell,
And write your stories who can tell?

Scarlet Scribbles in the Eldertree

Beneath the twisting, gnarled bark,
The scribbles shine, a crimson mark.
A story waits in tangles tight,
Within the heart of ancient night.

The Eldertree, with branches wide,
Holds laughter, love, and sorrow's tide.
Each leaf a tale, each root a bind,
Where woven dreams and truth unwind.

In whispered tales of joy and woe,
Scarlet ink starts to freely flow.
A tapestry of life appears,
Embracing hearts, dissolving fears.

Through time and space, the echoes sing,
Of wonder wrought from everything.
With every stroke upon the grain,
The stories bless both joy and pain.

So linger close and mark the page,
In every word, let ancients gauge.
The Eldertree shall guard your heart,
In every scribble, life shall start.

The Mystique of Ruby Glyphs

Upon the walls where shadows creep,
The ruby glyphs in silence leap.
Transcendent signs of ages past,
With secrets held, forever cast.

The night unfurls its inky veil,
A symphony of whispered trail.
Each symbol glows, a tale ignites,
Against the dark, a dance of lights.

In hidden groves, where magic dwells,
The ruby ink casts ancient spells.
To speak their truth, just dare to dream,
And find the light within the seam.

As tendrils weave through time and thought,
The mystery unfolds, lessons taught.
With every glance, the heart aligns,
In ruby depths, the spirit twines.

So seek the signs that fate bestows,
In every mark, the wisdom flows.
The mystique holds a boundless grace,
With ruby glyphs, you find your place.

Echoes of the Twilight Grove

In the hush of the evening's sigh,
Shadows waltz as the stars comply.
Whispers weave through the ancient trees,
Carried on a soft, enchanted breeze.

Moonlight dapples the forest floor,
Setting secrets by a hidden door.
Where wishes linger and dreams ignite,
In the arms of the gentle night.

Twilight's breath stirs the leaves awake,
While echoes murmur of choices made.
Each rustling sound, a tale retold,
In the cryptic glade, where time turns cold.

Mysteries swirl in that shadowed place,
Fleeting glimpses of a fairy's grace.
The twilight holds its breath in wait,
For the dawn to open love's small gate.

An invitation to the brave and true,
To wander where the wildflowers grew.
Hearts entwined with the moon's soft gleam,
Awake in the echo of a dream.

Signatures Left by Luminous Fae

Beneath the veils of twilight's charm,
Fae weave their magic, twinkling warm.
Their laughter dances on air so light,
Painting the world with shards of bright.

Each step they take leaves a glow,
A shimmering path where few may go.
Curious hearts may follow the thread,
To secrets kept in whispers said.

Little lanterns drifting on high,
Glow like dreams that never die.
They flit between branches, elusive and fair,
Encouraging wishes tangled in air.

In softest glens where shadows play,
Luminous whispers lead the way.
On petals soft, they leave their mark,
Guiding the lost through the dark.

The tapestry glows with stories rare,
Each thread a promise that lingers there.
In the heart of night, hopes intertwine,
With signatures signed by fae divine.

The Enigma of the Petal Script

A whisper caught in the evening dew,
Petals scripting a tale anew.
In colors vibrant, tales unfold,
Of wondrous spells and secrets bold.

Each blossom cradles a hidden verse,
A rhythm soft, a gentle curse.
The breeze carries tales of yore,
Across the glade's forgotten floor.

Woven words in nature's hand,
Translating dreams in silent strands.
A code entwined in vine and thorn,
Where echoes of magic are reborn.

In twilight's embrace, the petals dance,
Inviting souls to take a chance.
To read the script upon the ground,
And find the truths that can astound.

When moonlight stretches through boughs above,
Unlocking the language of hidden love.
In softest hues, let your spirit soar,
And unveil the world you've yearned for.

Legends of the Twilight Bloom

In the hush of dusk, the legends breathe,
Twilight blooms beneath the eaves.
Whispers rise with the evening mist,
Stories of hope that none can resist.

Petals unfurl with a spellbound grace,
Holding dreams in their delicate lace.
The nightingale sings of forgotten lore,
Of kingdoms lost and battles sore.

Through tangled woods where shadows gleam,
Twilight blooms in a silvery dream.
With every flutter, the past comes alive,
As ancient secrets begin to thrive.

Once a tale spun in gentle sighs,
Now etched in stars, where magic lies.
A journey awaits for the brave at heart,
Among the blooms where the legends start.

So wander forth into night's embrace,
Seek the tales hidden in time and space.
For in the twilight, the stories loom,
And life finds strength in the twilight bloom.